Bermuda Iconic Travel Guide 2025

Everything To Know In This Beautiful Island, Horseshoe and Elbow Beaches, Dinning and Luxury Accommodation with Reference Map.

Tara D. Hayes

Copyright © 2024 by Tara D. Hayes

This book is a non-fiction work. All characters, incidents, and dialogue are based on the author's personal experiences, interviews, and research. Any resemblance to actual persons, living or dead, or events is purely coincidental.

While every effort has been made to provide accurate and up-to-date information, neither the author nor the publisher can be held liable for any errors or omissions or for any consequences resulting from the use of this information.

Table of Contents

Chapter One: Welcome to Bermuda.

1.1 Introduction: A paradise in the North Atlantic.

"The island wasn't like the ones on the rum maps, all buried gold and skull and crossbones. It was a place of pink sand, whispering palms, and water so clear it looked like the bottled sky." - Captain Don't Cry author Mark Zusak.

Close your eyes for a minute. Feel the warm sun caressing your skin as the lovely Atlantic wind whispers through your hair. Imagine yourself on a beach where the sand is a delicate pink, and the sea is a stunning mix of turquoise and sapphire. Welcome to Bermuda, a group of islands drifting in the expanse of the North Atlantic, where peace and adventure coexist.

This isn't just another beach vacation. Beyond the beautiful beaches, Bermuda provides a variety of experiences. Immerse yourself in the rich tapestry of history that unfolds in the picturesque village of St. George's, a UNESCO World Heritage Site embellished with pastel-coloured buildings whispering stories of bygone eras. Descend into the Crystal Caves, where natural formations carved by time create a world of sparkling stalactites and stalagmites. Discover the lively Bermudian culture, a unique combination of British, African, Portuguese, and Native American influences shown in the kindness of the people and the pace of their lives.

Are you a sun worshipper who wants to dissolve into the arms of everlasting relaxation? Bermuda's beautiful beaches beckon. Do you seek the excitement of discovering vibrant underwater worlds? The island's magnificent coral reefs welcome your daring spirit. Perhaps history is whispering your name? Explore the old forts that serve as a reminder of the island's history. This travel guide is vital to discovering every aspect of this intriguing island.

So pack your bags, put on sunscreen, and get ready to enjoy a paradise unlike any other. Allow Bermuda to work its charm on you, a place where the rhythm of the water lulls you into peace and the spirit of adventure awakens your soul.

1.2 Fast Facts: Important facts about Bermuda

Bermuda beckons, but before you make a ship, here's a summary of vital information to guarantee a seamless and fantastic island experience:
Bermuda is an archipelago of around 181 islands rather than a single continent. The eight major islands are linked by bridges and causeways, making exploring simple. No matter where you go, you're only a mile from the ocean's embrace.

Currency Exchange: Bermuda's currency is the Bermudian Dollar (BMD), which has a fixed exchange rate with the U.S. Dollar (USD), with $1 equaling BMD 1. Credit cards are frequently accepted, although bringing some Bermudian cash is helpful for little transactions and taxi rides.

Calling from abroad: If you are travelling by phone, check with your carrier for foreign roaming costs. Alternatively, acquire a local SIM card upon arrival for more cost-effective communication.

Bermuda's electrical outlets are the same as those in the United States and Canada (120V, 60Hz). Hence, most

North American appliances do not need voltage converters to operate.

Bermuda's subtropical climate includes warm to scorching summers and moderate, windy winters. Pack for the sun, but don't forget a light jacket for the odd evening with a pleasant seaside breeze.

Dress Code Informal: Bermuda has a relaxed and informal dress code. Consider comfortable clothes for touring, swimwear for the beach, and light evening dress for eating out. Leave your formal attire home; Bermuda is about enjoying the island feel.

Tipping Etiquette: In Bermuda, tipping is comparable to that in the United States: 15-20% off meals, a few dollars for taxi trips, and a little gratuity for exemplary service providers.

Time Zone Traveler: Bermuda follows Atlantic Standard Time (AST), one hour ahead of Eastern Standard Time (EST) and four hours ahead of Pacific Standard Time.

Bermuda provides a duty-free refuge for shopping sprees. However, quantities are limited, so check allowances before purchasing luxury goods.

Safety first: Bermuda is a safe place with a low crime rate. However, it is always advisable to exercise caution. Keep valuables in hotel safes and be aware of your surroundings, particularly at night.

Healthy Habits: Bermuda has outstanding medical services, although basic travel insurance is usually suggested. Pack any necessary prescriptions, and remember that Bermuda gets a lot of sun, so reef-safe sunscreen is vital.

Hitting the Waves: Want to rent jet skis and explore the undersea world? Life jackets are required for most water activities in Bermuda. Safety comes first, always!

Sunday Slowdown: Sundays are quieter in Bermuda since many stores and businesses shut wholly or early. Plan your shopping trips accordingly.

Eco-conscious Traveler: Bermuda takes environmental responsibility very seriously. Many hotels implement water-saving programs, and single-use plastics are prohibited. Refill your water bottle and adopt a reusable lifestyle.

Language Lesson: You may hear certain Bermudian colloquialisms while English is the official language. Do not be shocked by expressions like "good morning, love" or "cracking good"; they are all part of the island's charm.

Driving on the Left: If you intend to hire a scooter (motorbike) to tour the island, be prepared for left-hand traffic. Before you leave, take your time and get to know the roads. Taxis are easily accessible and a safe option.

Bermuda's public bus system is fast and reasonably priced, linking the most significant regions. Purchase a bus pass for more accessible travel. Ferries are also provided for island hopping and picturesque tours.

Staying Connected: Most hotels have Wi-Fi connectivity, and public Wi-Fi hotspots are available in some regions. Check with your service provider for data roaming possibilities in Bermuda.

Island Essentials: Bring comfortable walking shoes for exploration, a swimsuit for beach days, a hat for sun protection, and a reusable water bottle to remain hydrated. An adaptor for foreign plugs is unnecessary, but bring your camera to capture those postcard-perfect moments!

With these practical must-know recommendations, you'll be ready to begin your wonderful Bermudian vacation. Allow the island's enchantment to work its spell, and prepare to make memories that will last a lifetime!

1.3 Transportation: Flights, cruises, and ferries to Bermuda

So you've decided to visit Bermuda's lovely beaches, which is excellent! Now it's time to plan your arrival. This island paradise welcomes you with open arms and provides a range of transportation alternatives to fit your travel style and budget. Fasten your seatbelt (or life jacket!) as we examine the many methods to get to Bermuda.

Taking flight:

Bermuda's principal international airport, allows for quick arrival. ***L.F-Wade International Airport (BDA)*** is conveniently situated in the northeast parish of St. Georges. Several airlines provide year-round travel to Bermuda, making selecting a trip that suits your schedule simple. Here are several prominent carriers connecting you to the island:

- **American Airlines** has regular flights from major US hubs such as Charlotte (CLT), John F. Kennedy International Airport (JFK) in New York, and Miami International Airport (MIA).

- **Bermuda Air**, Bermuda's native airline, offers accessible connections from many East Coast locations, including Boston (BOS), Fort Lauderdale (FLL), Hamilton, Ontario (YHM), and Toronto Pearson International Airport (YYZ).

- Delta Airlines has flights between Atlanta (ATL) and JFK in New York.

- JetBlue offers year-round service from Boston (BOS), with flights moving to a four-day schedule in November.

- **United Airlines:** Take a United trip from Newark Liberty International Airport (EWR) in New Jersey. Service is reduced to four days weekly in January and February, with daily flights resumed in March.

Cost considerations: Flight rates vary based on the time of year, airline, and booking time. A round-trip ticket typically costs a few hundred to well over a thousand dollars, depending on your origin location and travel dates. Be a wise traveller:

- Examine costs.
- Consider travelling during the week (typically cheaper than at weekends).
- Book your journey in advance for the best bargains.

Cruise into Paradise:

Consider taking a cruise ship for a more relaxed arrival. Several major cruise companies make Bermuda a port of stop, enabling you to spend a relaxing day or two discovering the island's beauty before continuing your journey. Here are some major cruise companies that incorporate Bermuda in their itineraries:

- **Royal Caribbean International:** Set sail with Royal Caribbean and immerse yourself in a magnificent island getaway. The costs vary based on the route and cabin chosen.
- **Celebrity Cruises:** Enjoy the sophisticated luxury of Celebrity Cruises when visiting Bermuda. Cruise costs vary depending on the route and stateroom selected.
- When visiting Bermuda, take advantage of Norwegian Cruise Line's Freestyle Cruising,

which allows you more freedom and flexibility. Pricing varies according to the schedule and requested accommodations.

Ferrying between islands:

While ferries are not a direct route from mainland locations, they can provide a quick and picturesque means to move between Bermuda's numerous islands once you arrive. The public ferry system offers a dependable and cost-effective way to travel between islands or major cities. Here's a brief overview of the ferry system:

- **The Ferry Schedule:** Ferries run daily, with various frequencies depending on the route. The current ferry schedule and route details are available on the Bermuda Tourism website.
- **Fare and Zones:** Ferry costs vary per zone, ranging from $3.50 to $5 for each journey. Exact change and pre-purchased tickets are accepted. If you want to use the ferries often, consider obtaining a Transportation Pass for consecutive days.

Choosing your path:

The best method to go to Bermuda is based on your choices and budget. For a speedy and straightforward arrival, fly straight into L.F. Wade International Airport, the place to go. Cruising is a sumptuous and peaceful experience, enabling you to combine your Bermuda stay with travel to other countries. For those already in the area, ferries provide a gorgeous and economical method to travel between Bermuda's intriguing islands.

Bermuda welcomes visitors regardless of how they arrive. So pack your luggage, book your passage, and prepare to find your own North Atlantic paradise.

1.4 Island Orientation: Parishes, Regions, and Moving Around

Bermuda may be a collection of islands, but traversing them is simple! This lovely archipelago has nine parishes with distinct personalities and charm. Let's get you started before you go on your Bermudian adventure:

Parishes Unveiled:

St. George's is Bermuda's oldest and UNESCO World Heritage Site town. Cobblestone streets adorned with pastel-coloured houses, old forts, and fascinating museums await your discovery.

Hamilton, Bermuda's central city, is alive with activity. Explore the shops on Front Street, take a walk in the lovely Queen Elizabeth Park, or enjoy the harbour vistas.

Southampton: This south coast parish is a popular destination for sunbathers. Relax on the famed Horseshoe Bay Beach, a crescent of pink sand surrounded by blue seas. Explore the Bermuda Underwater Exploration Institute to learn about the island's aquatic life.

Warwick: Warwick offers opportunities for adventure. Kayak through crystal-clear mangrove bays, golf on championship courses, or explore the Crystal Caves.

Sandys: History nerds, rejoice! Sandys is home to forts from the 17th century. Visit the Wreck Hill Nature Reserve for a gorgeous stroll, or explore the Bermuda Railway Trail for a unique island view.

Paget's luxurious lifestyle defines him. He indulges at world-class spas, tees off on groomed greens at luxury golf courses, and relaxes on beautiful beaches.

Pembroke: This centre parish combines history and natural beauty. Visit the Dockyard, a naval wonder, or the Bermuda Botanical Gardens, which have a vivid display of vegetation.

Devonshire is a nature lover's delight! It has undulating hills, peaceful coves, and the headquarters of the Bermuda National Trust, which provides access to protected natural areas.

Smith's: This westernmost parish is renowned for its stunning coastline and secret coves. Explore the Leamington Caves, a network of underground caverns, or hike the Bermuda National Trust trails.

Getting Around Easily:

Now that you have a sense for Bermuda's parishes let's look at your transit options:

- **Public buses:** Bermuda's efficient public bus system provides an inexpensive method to go across the island. Purchase a Transportation Pass for unrestricted travel within a specific timeframe. Download the Bermuda Public Transport app to get real-time bus arrival information.
- **Ferries:** Board a boat to visit various parishes or take a picturesque tour between islands. Ferries run every day at varied intervals depending on the route.
- **Rental Scooters:** For the daring, hiring a scooter (motorbike) is a fun and versatile way to move about. Remember that Bermuda travels on the left side of the road, so ensure you know how to navigate before heading out.
- **Taxis:** Taxis are frequently accessible for quick point-to-point transportation, particularly if carrying baggage or touring after dark. Fares are metered, so you'll know what you're paying upfront.
- **Bicycle Rentals:** Pedal around the island at your speed. Most parishes offer bike rentals, a healthy and environmentally responsible way to discover Bermuda's beauty.

Top Tips for Moving Around:

- Download a map of Bermuda or use a GPS navigation app to help you get around.
- If you want to explore extensively, consider purchasing a Transportation Pass, which allows unrestricted public bus and boat travel.
- Be aware of traffic restrictions, particularly if hiring a scooter. Always wear your helmet!
- Taxis are a handy choice, but expect higher rates than public transit.
- Consider walking or cycling short distances, particularly in picturesque regions, to appreciate the island's splendour fully.

With some preparation and this guidance, exploring Bermuda will be a snap. So, select your parish and your means of transportation, and prepare to discover the enchantment of this enchanting island!

1.5 A Brief History: From Shipwrecks to British Colonies.

Bermuda has a fascinating history, weaved through shipwrecks, exploration, and colonial impact. Let's explore the island's intriguing history and learn about the events that formed this mesmerizing paradise:

Early Encounters:

While Bermuda was likely uninhabited for most of human history, the island's first reported contact occurred in 1503. Juan de Bermúdez, a Spanish adventurer, discovered the archipelago and named it for its fate. However, the islands were mainly undiscovered and unclaimed for almost a century.

Shipwreck on Paradise:

In 1609, destiny intervened. The notorious Sea Venture, leader of a force destined for Virginia, sank on Bermuda's reefs. Miraculously, everyone on board escaped, including Sir George Somers, the future governor of Virginia. This accidental shipwreck signalled the start of Bermuda's permanent colonization.

Founding Fathers:

The shipwrecked colonists were inventive and persistent, salvaging materials from the Sea Venture and building basic shelters. They finally established the first permanent colony in St. George's, named after their Captain, Sir George Somers. Thus, the English colonization of Bermuda started.

The Virginia Company:

The Virginia Company first administered Bermuda, seeing the island's potential as a source of food and supplies for their mainland colony. Settlers started farming the area and building a primitive infrastructure.

The Somers Isles Company:

The Somers Isles Company was founded in 1615, ushering in a new era. This firm obtained a royal charter, giving it power over Bermuda's growth. The corporation specialized in tobacco cultivation, shipbuilding, and constructing a self-sufficient colony.

The arrival of Africans

While the early inhabitants were mostly English, the entrance of enslaved Africans in 1616 marked a low point in Bermuda's history. Africans were forced into work, and they contributed significantly to the island's growth. Their impact on Bermudian culture and society is unmistakable.

A crown colony:

Bermuda became a crown colony ruled directly by the British throne when the Somers Isles Company's contract was dissolved in 1684. This move resulted in a more significant military presence, emphasizing Bermuda's strategic position in the Atlantic.

American Revolutionary War:

During the American Revolution, Bermuda's status as a British colony put it in peril. The island became essential for British naval operations, with repeated encounters with American privateers.

Civil War and Beyond:

Bermuda was strategically positioned once again during the American Civil War. The island was a necessary refuelling and resupply location for Confederate blockade runners. Following the war, Bermuda flourished as a British colony, eventually shifting to a more critical position in tourism and international commerce in the twentieth century.

A Legacy Unfolding:

Today, Bermuda is a fascinating combination of its rich past. The island's architecture, fortifications, and cultural traditions bear witness to its discovery, shipwreck, and colonial history. As you visit Bermuda, remember the compelling tales woven into its very fabric, which serve as a tribute to perseverance, human connection, and the island paradise's continuing appeal.

Chapter 2: Plan Your Trip

2.1 When to Go: Seasons, Weather Patterns, and Best Time to Visit

"Choose a season that suits your soul." - Anonymous

Bermuda welcomes visitors annually, but your vacation plans determine the best time to visit. This intriguing island has a subtropical climate with significant seasonal fluctuations accommodating various interests. Look at Bermuda's weather trends and choose the best time for your fantasy island getaway.

Spring Symphony (March to May):

Spring paints Bermuda with a bright hue. The average temperature rises to a comfortable 76°F (24°C), with cool coastal breezes to mitigate the heat. This shoulder season has various benefits:

- **Fewer crowds:** Spring provides a break from the peak summer throngs, allowing for a more leisurely exploration of the island's beauty.
- **Pleasant Weather:** The days are delightfully warm, ideal for seeing historical sites, trekking

picturesque routes, or participating in water activities without the burning summer heat.

- **Whaley Good Time:** March marks the conclusion of the spiny lobster season, providing a unique chance to enjoy this local delicacy before it goes on vacation until September.

Summer Sizzle (June to August):

Bermuda's summer is characterized by sunlight and average temperatures of 85°F (29°C). This is peak season, teeming with activity and providing the classic beach holiday experience.

- Summer in Bermuda is excellent for swimming, snorkelling, diving, and soaking up the sun on the island's famous pink-sand beaches.
- Summer has exciting activities like sailing competitions, cultural festivities, and lively entertainment alternatives.
- **Water Sports Paradise:** Warm waters and calm seas provide ideal conditions for a wide range of water sports, including kayaking, paddleboarding, jet skiing, and deep-sea fishing.

Autumn's Embrace (September to November):

As summer fades, Bermuda settles into a relaxed autumn embrace. The people start to dwindle, and the island takes on a peaceful charm:

- **Hurricane Season:** It is vital to know that Bermuda's hurricane season runs from June to November. While there is no assurance, the possibility of tropical storms should be considered now.
- **Golden Light:** The fall months provide a stunning display of golden light, ideal for taking postcard-worthy photos of the island's scenery.
- **Cheaper prices:** Hotels and vacation cottages often offer cheaper prices during autumn, making Bermuda affordable.

Winter Wonderland (December to February):

Winter brings moderate weather to Bermuda, with average temperatures around 65°F (18°C). This is the quietest time to come and provides a calm escape:

- **Escape the Crowds:** The best time to appreciate Bermuda's peacefulness is during the winter. Enjoy uncrowded beaches, historical sights, and a laid-back island lifestyle.
- **Festive Delights:** The Christmas season adds a touch of enchantment to Bermuda with festive decorations, unique activities, and a cheerful environment.
- Winter is traditionally considered the off-season, with the lowest prices on flights and lodgings.

The Perfect Choice:

So, what is the ideal time to visit Bermuda? The answer depends on your vacation aspirations. Summer is the season for seaside enjoyment and vivid activity. Spring and October are perfect for a relaxing getaway and a low-cost excursion. And if you want a calm winter trip, the off-season has excellent appeal. Bermuda offers a fantastic experience that awaits discovery at any time of year.

2.2 Visa and Entry Requirements: What You Need To Enter Bermuda

Bermuda greets you with open arms, but before you depart on your island trip, be sure you have everything for a smooth arrival. Here's an overview of the visas and entrance criteria you'll need to consider:

Visa-Free Paradise (For the Most):

The good news is that most nations do not need a visa to visit Bermuda for tourism reasons. Suppose you are a citizen of the United States, Canada, the United Kingdom, most European Union countries, Australia, New Zealand, or a handful of other countries. In that case, you may breathe a sigh of relief. With valid documents, you will be given access for up to 180 days.

Double-check to be sure.

However, checking visa requirements with your local Bermudian consulate or embassy is always advisable before your travel. Here are some resources that can assist you:

- Bermuda Immigration Department website: https://www.gov.bm/department/immigration.
- Interactive Visa Checker: https://travel.gc.ca/destinations/bermuda (The Canadian Government's website includes a user-friendly visa checker tool; although not Bermuda-specific, it may be a helpful starting point.)

What You Will Need:

The following are the essential papers you'll need to provide upon arriving in Bermuda:

- **Valid Passport:** Your passport must be valid for at least six months after your anticipated departure from Bermuda.
- **Proof of Onward or Return Travel:** Prepare to present immigration authorities with a confirmed return airline ticket or other paperwork for onward travel to another place.
- **Completed Arrival Card:** Upon arrival from your flight, you will be given an arrival card. Please fill it out entirely with your trip details and contact information.

Additional considerations:

While not required, having the following papers readily accessible might speed up the entrance procedure.

- **Proof of Accommodation:** A hotel reservation confirmation or rental agreement showing your stay in Bermuda may be helpful.
- **Travel Insurance** is not required. However, peace of mind is strongly recommended during unexpected occurrences.

Entering With a Minor:

If you're travelling with children under 18, ensure you have a copy of their birth certificate and a notarized letter of permission if they go alone or with one parent.

Remember:

Entry criteria are subject to change. Therefore, it's critical to remain current with the most recent information from official sources. With the correct papers and a little planning, you'll be whisked through Bermuda immigration and on your way to seeing this beautiful island paradise.

2.3 Currency and Money Matters: The Bermudian Dollar (BMD) and Budgeting Tips

Bermuda has a dual-currency system, with the Bermudian Dollar (BMD) ruling supreme. The U.S. Dollar (USD) is commonly accepted on the island, typically at a one-to-one exchange rate. This section looks into the complexities of Bermudian money and provides budgeting advice to guarantee a financially successful island getaway.

Bermudian Dollar:

Bermuda's national currency is the Bermudian Dollar (BMD), issued in coin and banknote denominations ($1, $5, $10, $25, $50, and $100). These notes have a distinctive design that depicts the island's flora and wildlife, historical sites, and the Queen of England. While U.S. dollars are generally accepted, bringing some Bermudian currency for smaller purchases, taxis, and buses is advisable since some merchants may not have easily accessible change for high USD amounts.

Exchanging currencies:

Banks, airport currency exchange kiosks, and certain hotels provide currency exchange services. Rates may vary somewhat, so compare before exchanging significant funds. ATMs that accept Bermudian dollars are also readily accessible over the island. However, verify with your bank about any possible overseas transaction costs.

Credit cards and travellers' checks:

Major credit cards like Visa, MasterCard, and American Express are frequently accepted in Bermuda, especially at hotels, restaurants, and giant retailers. Traveller's checks are less prevalent, and acceptance may be restricted. If you opt to utilize traveller's checks, be sure they are denominated in U.S. dollars for ease of usage.

Budgeting in Bermuda:

Depending on your travel preferences, Bermuda may be a low-cost vacation or a refuge for luxury shopping. Here are some financial suggestions to keep in mind:

- **Accommodation:** Bermuda offers a variety of lodging alternatives, from low-cost guesthouses to luxury resorts. When booking your accommodation, consider your requirements and preferences.
- **Dining:** Bermuda's restaurants cater to all budgets. Fine dining experiences cost more, while neighbourhood cafes and informal restaurants are cheaper. To save money on meals, consider self-catering at your hotel.
- Bermuda offers a wide range of free and low-cost activities. Discover public beaches, trek gorgeous trails, explore historical sites, or relax and enjoy

the island's splendour. Paid activities like diving expeditions, boat cruises, and golfing are available at an extra expense.

- Public buses and ferries provide a quick and economical option to get throughout the island. Consider obtaining a transit pass to ensure limitless travel throughout your stay. Taxis are more costly, but they provide a handy point-to-point service. Renting a scooter might be entertaining, but consider the rental and petrol costs.

By following these recommendations and arranging your trip ahead of time, you may ensure a financially rewarding and delightful Bermuda holiday.

2.4 Packing Essentials: What to Bring on Your Bermuda Adventure

Bermuda entices with its sunlight, blue seas, and alluring charm. Packing the appropriate items is crucial for a pleasant and hassle-free vacation. Here's a thorough advice about what to pack for your fantastic Bermudian getaway:

Clothing for Every Occasion:

- **Sun Protection Essentials:** Bermuda has a subtropical temperature, so bring lots of sunscreen (reef-safe kinds are recommended!), a wide-brimmed hat, and UV-protective sunglasses.

- **Beach Bliss:** Swimsuits, cover-ups, beach towels, and quick-drying shoes are required for sunbathing on Bermuda's beautiful beaches.
- Comfortable walking shoes are essential for touring historical places, trekking picturesque paths, and traversing quaint villages: pack light, breathable apparel such as cotton t-shirts, shorts, and sundresses.
- **Light Jacket:** Evenings may be pleasant with coastal breezes, so bring a light jacket or sweater for versatile layering.
- **Evening attire:** Although Bermuda is mainly casual, certain restaurants may have a dress code. Pack a light dress or pants with a collared shirt for formal dining occasions.

Essentials for All Travelers:

- Pack comfy pyjamas or loungewear to ensure a good night's sleep after your activities.
- Pack adequate underwear and socks for the whole vacation. Quick-drying choices are suitable for tropical climates.
- **Toiletries:** Bring your necessary toiletries, but remember that most hotels provide basic amenities such as shampoo, conditioner, and body wash. Consider using travel-sized containers to conserve room.

- **Personal Medication:** Pack any drugs you need, ensuring they are in their original labelled containers.
- **Electronics:** Remember your phone charger, a portable power bank (if necessary), and any photography equipment you want to use to record Bermuda memories. Most North American appliances do not need an adaptor since Bermuda utilizes the same electrical outlets (120V, 60Hz).

Bonus Bermuda-specific essentials:

- **Reusable Water Bottle:** Keeping hydrated is critical under the Bermudian heat. A reusable water bottle may help you save money and minimize plastic waste.
- If you want to participate in water sports, a dry bag will protect your valuables from splashes and even downpours.
- **Plug Adapter (Optional)**: While most North American appliances do not need a universal adapter, one may come in useful if you are going from another location with a different plug type.

Remember:

Before you pack, check your airline's luggage limit and regulations. Consider layering garments to adjust to Bermuda's changing temps. By bringing these necessities, you'll be well-prepared to undertake your Bermuda journey and make lasting memories on this beautiful island paradise.

2.5 Accommodation: Resorts, hotels, guest homes, and vacation rentals.

"Paradise isn't a place, it's a feeling." — Unknown.

Bermuda beckons and an island symphony awaits your arrival. However, before your island journey, you must choose your ideal haven. Bermuda has diverse hotel alternatives, from opulent resorts to lovely guesthouses, to suit every taste and budget. Let's look at your refuge possibilities:

Luxurious Lakeside Living: The *Fairmont Hamilton Princess* (https://www.fairmont.com/hamilton-bermuda/) offers unrivalled luxury. This historic hotel, located on the beaches of Hamilton Harbour, offers magnificent guest suites, world-class restaurants, a revitalizing spa, and a private beach club. Expect to spend more than $1,000 per night for a deluxe getaway.

Fairmont Hamilton Princess

Oceanfront Oasis: Experience beachside paradise at the ***Hamilton Princess & Beach Club, A Fairmont Managed Hotel*** (https://www.fairmont.com/hamilton-bermuda/). This vast resort has breathtaking ocean views, various pools, tennis courts, a watersports centre, and all the amenities you'd expect from a world-renowned brand. Rates usually start around $700 per night.

Hamilton Princess & Beach Club, A Fairmont-Managed Hotel

Romantic Getaway: *The Reefs Resort & Club* (https://www.thereefs.com/gallery) on Bermuda's south coast offers intimacy and elegance. This adults-only paradise offers magnificent beachfront rooms, delicious restaurants, and a relaxing spa. Nightly prices here might reach $800 or more.

The Reefs Resort and Club

Family Fun: Spend quality time with your loved ones at the ***Cambridge Beaches Resort & Spa*** (https://www.cambridgebeaches.com/) on Somerset Island. This spacious resort has a choice of lodging options, a specialized children's club, many pools, and a beachfront position ideal for sandcastle building and splashing in the surf. Expect prices to start around $500 per night.

Cambridge Beaches Resort and Spa

A Historical Escape: Travel back in time at the ***Rosedon Hotel*** (https://rosedonhotel.com/), a quaint hotel steeped in Bermuda's rich past. This historic house in the centre of St. George's combines Bermudian hospitality with contemporary comforts. Rates here are often lower, beginning at roughly $300 per night.

Rosedon Hotel

Budget-Friendly Charm: Check out Bermuda's guesthouses for a pleasant and economical stay. These family-run enterprises provide a more personal experience and an opportunity to engage with the local Bermudian culture. Expect to spend between $150 and $200 per night for decent accommodation with a flavour of local warmth.

Home Away from Home: Enjoy solitude and freedom with a holiday property in Bermuda. Alternatives are available, from beachfront condominiums to private cottages, enabling you to tailor your Bermudian experience. Rental fees vary according to the size, location, and facilities provided.

Finding the Perfect Match:

Bermuda has a varied choice of lodging alternatives to meet the needs of every tourist. Find your ideal Bermudian refuge by considering your budget, vacation style, and required facilities. Whether you want beachside luxury, historic charm, or a quiet home away from home, the island has a hideaway waiting for you. So, start arranging your ideal getaway and prepare to explore the magic that lies in Bermuda!

2.6 Moving Around: Buses, Ferries, Taxis, Scooters, and Rental Cars

Bermuda may be a collection of islands, but getting around is simple! This picturesque archipelago has a well-developed transit infrastructure, so you can easily visit every area. Here's your guide to navigating Bermuda's beauty, from affordable buses to thrilling scooter rides:

Public Buses: The Affordable Explorer.

Bermuda's public bus system, affectionately known as the "buses," is a safe, quick, and inexpensive means of getting around the island. The brightly coloured buses run all day, with routes linking the most significant cities and parishes. Fares are a set charge, often between $4 and $6 for each journey, payable with exact change or a bought transit ticket. Download the "Bermuda Public Transport" app for real-time bus arrivals and route planning.

Ferries: Island hopping with scenic views.

Get aboard a boat to see various parishes or take a picturesque journey across the islands. The Bermuda Ferry Company runs many routes, including the Hamilton-Dockyard Ferry, the Hamilton-St. George's Ferry, and the Cross Sound Ferry, which links the main island with the distant St. David's Island. Ferry costs vary by route and distance, ranging from $5 to $20 per trip. Tickets may be purchased at ferry ports or online in advance.

Taxis provide convenient point-to-point transportation.

Taxis are widely accessible for easy point-to-point transportation, particularly if carrying baggage or touring after dark. Taxi stalls may be found near hotels, cruise ship ports, and popular tourist destinations. Fares are metered, so you'll know what you're paying upfront. Taxis are often more costly than buses or ferries, with rates ranging from $10 to $15 for short journeys and rising with distance. Some taxi firms provide flat prices for pre-booked trips. Here are some prominent Bermuda Taxi Companies:

- Weir's Taxi Service: https://ridebermuda.com/ (renowned for its courteous drivers and clean taxis).
- AAT Taxi (https://ridebermuda.com)
- People's Taxi: https://ridebermuda.com.

Scooters: The Adventurer's Spirit

For the brave, renting a scooter (motorbike) is a fun and flexible way to navigate Bermuda. Remember that Bermuda travels on the left side of the road, so ensure you know how to navigate before heading out. Scooter rentals are available in most parishes, with fees generally ranging from $75 to $100 per day (excluding petrol). Ensure you have a valid driver's license and always wear a helmet. Here are some reliable scooter rental companies:

- Oleander Cycles: https://www.oleandercycles.bm/ (located in Paget and offers an extensive range of scooters)
- Paradise Rentals: https://www.airbnb.com/rooms/10846337 (provides scooter rentals at several spots across the island).
- Motorscooters Bermuda: https://www.bermuda.com/transportation/scooter -rentals/ (based in Hamilton and focuses on customer service).

Rental Cars: A Notable Exception.

Unlike other island resorts, Bermuda limits automobile rentals to residents exclusively. This is done to reduce traffic congestion and encourage more environmentally friendly modes of transportation. However, electric car rentals are becoming more widely accessible, providing a more ecologically aware option. Keep a look out for future advancements in this area!

Choosing Your Perfect Ride

The best means of transportation depends on your budget, travel style, and desired amount of flexibility. Buses and ferries are a low-cost option to explore, while taxis provide handy point-to-point transportation. Scooters give an exciting way to explore the island at your leisure, whilst rental automobiles (currently prohibited) enable complete freedom of movement. With so many alternatives available, you're sure to find the ideal method to traverse Bermuda's charm and discover the hidden jewels of this beautiful island paradise.

Chapter 3: Revealing Bermuda's Beauty

3.1 Hitting the Beach: Horseshoe Bay, Elbow Beach, and Hidden Coves

"The cure for anything is salt water: sweat, tears, or the sea." — Isadora Duncan.

Bermuda has a chain of beautiful beaches, each giving its taste of heaven. Dip your toes into the turquoise seas, relax on the distinctive pink beach, and let the warm Bermudian sun kiss your skin. Let's look at some of the best beaches for your island getaway:

Horseshoe Bay's Allure: Horseshoe Bay doesn't require an introduction. This crescent-shaped beach on Bermuda's south coast is a picture-perfect scene. The powdery pink beach spreads along a tranquil bay with crystal-clear seas, ideal for swimming, snorkelling, and relaxing in the sun. Umbrellas, loungers, and water sports equipment may be rented on the beach. Expect crowds, particularly during high season, but Horseshoe Bay's beauty is unquestionable.

Horseshoe Bay, Bermuda

Elbow Beach's Expanse: Elbow Beach, located on Bermuda's southwest side, has a lengthy and impressive shoreline. The pink sand here is somewhat coarser than at Horseshoe Bay, and the waves are more active, making it perfect for boogie boarding or body surfing. Elbow Beach is divided into numerous portions, some open to the public and others owned by seaside hotels. Find the ideal location to relax, soak up the sun, or participate in water sports.

Elbow Beach, Bermuda.

Church Bay's Snorkeling Haven: Visit Bermuda's south-central coast to explore Church Bay, a popular snorkelling destination. The quiet, clear waters teem with colourful fish and magnificent coral reefs, ready to be discovered. Rent snorkelling gear from beach vendors and go on an undersea excursion. Church Bay also has a crescent of pink sand and a laid-back ambience, ideal for a peaceful beach vacation.

Church Bay, Bermuda.

Hidden Gems Await:

Bermuda is a haven for people seeking a private hideaway, with hidden coves and secret beaches. Here are a handful to add to your exploring list.

Warwick Long Beach is located on Bermuda's south coast. It has a lengthy expanse of pink sand and tranquil waves. The beach has public access points and is well-known for its exceptional windsurfing conditions.

John Smith's Bay: This south coast beach has tranquil seas and a laidback environment. Families will like the availability of public toilets, changing facilities, and food sellers.

South Coast Park: Visit Bermuda's south coast and find South Shore Park, a public beach complete with a snack stand, bathrooms, and lifeguards on duty during peak season. The tranquil waters are great for swimming, and the park has a playground for youngsters.

Achilles Bay: Tucked away in Southampton Parish, Achilles Bay offers a private beach experience. Its calm waters and gorgeous surroundings make it an ideal location for a peaceful retreat.

Tobacco Bay Beach, located in St. George's Parish, is known for its stunning rock formations, attractive tidal pools, and rich history as a historic pirate hangout. The beach itself is a combination of pink sand and limestone stones, creating a distinct mood. There is an entry charge, but the exploring options and vibrant atmosphere make it well worth visiting.

Tobacco Bay Beach, Bermuda.

Beach Bliss Beyond the Sand:

Bermuda's beaches offer more than sunshine and sand. Many have concession kiosks that sell refreshments and snacks. Beach rentals include umbrellas, loungers, water sports equipment, and stand-up paddleboards or kayaks for exploring the coastline. The majority of prominent beaches have public toilets and changing facilities. During the peak season, several beaches have lifeguards on duty.

Finding the Perfect Beach:

Whether you want a bustling ambience, a private escape, or a beach ideal for snorkelling activities, Bermuda has a beach for you. So, pack your swimsuit, beach towel, and spirit of adventure and discover the beauty of Bermuda's gorgeous beaches!

3.2 Underwater Activities: Snorkeling, Diving, and Shipwreck Exploration

Bermuda's blue seas are more than simply stunning; they also serve as a doorway to a fascinating undersea world. Bermuda, teeming with colourful fish, brilliant coral reefs, and fascinating shipwrecks, provides an abundance of underwater thrills for divers of all skill levels. Let's look at the possibilities for discovering Bermuda's intriguing depths:

Snorkeling Paradise: Even if you've never used a mask and fins before, Bermuda's calm, beautiful waters make snorkelling a must-try. The island has several snorkelling areas rich with marine life. Visit Horseshoe Bay, Church Bay, or John Smith's Bay for easy access to spectacular coral reefs and schools of colourful fish. Most beaches provide snorkel gear, but you may also bring your own. As you glide over the crystal-clear waters, look for angelfish, parrotfish, butterflyfish, and other marine treasures.

Snorkelling paradise.

Dive Deeper: Bermuda offers a world of undersea adventure for trained divers. The island has nearly 300 shipwrecks, some dating back centuries, providing insight into Bermuda's rich marine past. Popular wreck diving destinations include the HMS Challenger, a Royal

Navy vessel that went aground in 1836, and the National Trust Wreck Trail, an underwater sculpture park filled with marine life. Dive operators on the island provide guided dives for divers of all skill levels, assuring a safe and memorable underwater excursion.

Diving Deeper

Underwater Photography:
1. Capture the enchantment of Bermuda's underwater realm through photography. Whether you're an experienced photographer or just starting, the beautiful coral reefs and colourful fish provide limitless opportunities to capture breathtaking photographs.
2. Purchase a waterproof camera housing or ask about rentals from diving operators.

3. Remember to change your camera settings for underwater photography to capture the rich colours and details of this fascinating environment.

Glass Bottom Boat Tours: If you're uncomfortable snorkelling or diving, a glass-bottom boat tour is an excellent opportunity to see Bermuda's underwater sights without getting wet. These cruises usually sail over coral reefs and shipwrecks, enabling you to watch marine life from the comfort of your boat. This is an excellent choice for families with small children or anybody seeking a peaceful approach to see Bermuda's underwater riches.

Glass Bottom Boat Tours.

Safety First:

Always emphasize safety while exploring Bermuda's aquatic ecosystem. If you're new to snorkelling or diving, join a friend or take a guided excursion. Be mindful of currents and use safe diving methods. Respect the maritime environment by not harming coral reefs or marine animals. By following these principles, you may have a safe and fun underwater excursion.

Underwater Adventures Await.

Bermuda provides something for everyone, whether you're an experienced diver, an inquisitive snorkeler, or want to see what's happening below. So pack your spirit of adventure, grab your snorkel or diving gear, and be ready to be captivated by Bermuda's underwater world.

3.3 Crystal Caves: Touring the Crystal and Fantasy Caves

Descend under Bermuda's surface and embark on a thrilling voyage via the Crystal and Fantasy Caves. These natural beauties, shaped by millions of years of rainfall erosion, will wow you with their ethereal beauty and geological marvels.

A Timeless Journey Begins: The Crystal and Fantasy Caves in Hamilton Parish is a must-see for anybody visiting Bermuda. Guided tours are available daily, taking you on a fascinating journey through magnificent subterranean churches. As you descend into the chilly depths, expect to be transported to another realm.

Crystal Cave: Where Light Dances on Water: The Crystal Cave is a breathtaking showcase of nature's creativity. Sunlight pours through gaps in the cave roof, revealing crystal-clear subterranean lakes and creating a magnificent interplay of light and water. Stalactites (formations hanging from the ceiling) and stalagmites (formations rising from the floor) cover the cave walls, resulting in an unearthly view. The pièce de résistance is the appropriately titled "Blue Hole," a deep, crystal-clear lake that reflects the sky's vivid blues.

Crystal Cave, Bermuda

Fantasy Cave: A Realm of Imagination: The Fantasy Cave provides a unique viewpoint on Bermuda's subsurface delights. Dry rooms studded with stalactites and stalagmites in various forms and sizes will pique your interest. Some formations resemble humans, while others depict flowing waterfalls or fantastical creatures. The fascinating rock formations and unusual lighting effects will make you feel like you've wandered into a mystical realm.

Fantasy Cave, Bermuda

A Glimpse into Bermuda's History: The Crystal Caves have captivated visitors for ages. The caverns may have been utilized for ritual reasons by the Cahowkia, a group of Native Bermudians. Two young boys exploring their garden uncovered the caverns in 1907, and they have since become a renowned tourist attraction.

A Timeless Adventure Awaits: A guided tour of the Crystal and Fantasy Caves lasts roughly 45 minutes. The caverns are open to the public every day, but reservations are suggested, particularly during high season. Wear comfortable shoes with adequate grip since the cave floor may be uneven and slippery in certain spots. The climate

within the caverns is cold year-round, so pack a light
jacket or sweater.

Unveiling Bermuda's Hidden Beauty

The Crystal and Fantasy Caves uniquely reveal
Bermuda's natural treasures. Explore this underground
world, marvel at the breathtaking formations, and
uncover the mesmerizing beauty underneath this magical
island's surface.

3.4 Historic St. George's: A UNESCO World Heritage Site with Charm

Travel back in time and see the lovely alleyways of St.
George's, Bermuda's UNESCO World Heritage Site. This
ancient town, established in 1612 as the first permanent
English colony in the New World, has a mesmerizing
combination of colourful architecture, rich history, and
marine charm. Let's discover the enchantment that awaits
you at St. George's:

A Town Rich in History: Walking along the cobblestone
lanes surrounded by pastel-coloured buildings, you'll be
transported to another period. St. George's has a rich
history, as seen by its forts, cathedrals, and other historic
sites. Don't miss attractions such as:

State House is the Commonwealth's oldest continually operational legislative building.

The unfinished church is a reminder of the island's early hardships.

Gates' Fort provides sweeping vistas and an intriguing look into Bermuda's military history.

St. Peter's Church is the oldest Anglican church in Bermuda, dating back to the 17th century.

A Cultural Tapestry: St. George's robust culture is reflected in its museums, art galleries, and local businesses. Explore the Bermuda National Museum to learn about the island's unique history, or visit the Bermuda Society of Arts to see local crafts and artwork. St. George's also has a variety of attractive stores that offer anything from Bermuda souvenirs to locally created crafts and designer items.

A Foodie's Paradise: Treat your taste buds to St. George's delectable culinary scene. Waterfront restaurants provide fresh seafood dishes with beautiful ocean views, while snug cafés and pubs offer the ideal setting for a tasty meal or a refreshing beverage. Don't miss the opportunity to eat Bermuda's trademark cuisine, fish chowder, a rich and savoury stew cooked with local fish, veggies, and spices.

Beyond the Town Walls: Explore beyond the town walls to see hidden treasures such as Tobacco Bay Beach, which has spectacular rock formations and attractive tidal pools. Take a lovely boat journey to the surrounding islands of St. David's and Cooper's Island Nature Reserve, which have breathtaking natural beauty and historical value.

St. George's is more than a historical site; it is also a charming town. Horse-drawn carriages provide a leisurely approach to tour the streets, and friendly inhabitants are always willing to tell anecdotes about their hometown. In the evenings, go to a seaside restaurant for live music or a neighbourhood bar to soak in the scene.

A Timeless Enchantment awaits:

St. George's is where history whispers through the cobblestones, and charm fills the air. So, put on your walking shoes, go on a trip through time, and enjoy the fascinating enchantment of this UNESCO World Heritage Site.

3.5 Cultural Gems: Museums, Forts, Lighthouses, and Architecture.

Bermuda's unique tale extends beyond its breathtaking beaches and blue seas. A vast cultural tapestry awaits, woven from historical sites, fascinating museums, and architectural treasures. Let us go on a voyage to uncover the island's cultural treasures:

Bermuda has several museums, each providing a unique glimpse into the island's history, culture, and natural environment. Here are several must-sees:

Bermuda National Museum: Located in St. George's, this extensive museum depicts Bermuda's remarkable history, from volcanic genesis to British colonization and beyond. Explore exhibitions about maritime history, cultural heritage and the island's distinct ecology.

Image of the Bermuda National Museum.

The National Gallery in Hamilton is a must-see for anybody interested in Bermuda's creative heritage. This distinguished organization has a vast collection of Bermudian and foreign art, ranging from historical treasures to modern works.

Step back in time and discover Bermuda's rich maritime legacy at the Dockyard Maritime Museum. This museum in the Royal Naval Dockyard has interactive displays, ship models, and historical relics that vividly depict Bermuda's naval heritage.

Image of the Dockyard Maritime Museum

Bermuda Underwater Exploration Institute: Discover the world under the waters at the Bermuda Underwater Exploration Institute. This intriguing museum has shipwreck relics, marine life exhibits, and interactive displays that will pique your interest in Bermuda's underwater domain.

Image of the Bermuda Underwater Exploration Institute

Guardians of the Coast: Forts and Lighthouses: Historic forts and lighthouses guard Bermuda's coasts, demonstrating the island's strategic significance. Explore: Fort St. Catherine: This magnificent 17th-century Fort in St. George's provides insight into Bermuda's role in protecting the British Empire. Walk around the ramparts, discover the underground corridors, and enjoy the spectacular ocean views.

Image of Fort St. Catherine in Bermuda.

Gibbs Hill Lighthouse: Climb to the top of Gibbs Hill Lighthouse, Bermuda's highest lighthouse, for stunning panoramic views of the island. This famous landmark, completed in 1846, has been crucial in nautical navigation for generations.

Image of Gibbs Hill Lighthouse in Bermuda.

St. David's Lighthouse: Located on Bermuda's easternmost point, St. David's Lighthouse provides breathtaking ocean views and the opportunity to tour a restored 19th-century lighthouse.

Image of St. David's Lighthouse in Bermuda.

Architectural Delights: Bermuda's architectural legacy combines British colonial influences with Bermudian creativity. As you go through the cities and villages, keep a look out for:

Traditional Bermuda houses: These delightful pastel-coloured houses, with their characteristic stepped roofs, are typical of Bermudian architecture. Many are wonderfully kept and provide insight into Bermuda's household life.

Fortifications: Stroll through Bermuda's fortifications, vestiges of the island's military history. The fortifications, bastions, and artillery batteries are evident in Bermuda's strategic importance.

Dockyard structures: The Royal Naval Dockyard has several ancient Bermuda stone structures. Explore the Commissioner's House, Clocktower, and Cooperage, admiring their architectural features and rich history.

A Cultural Journey Awaits: By exploring Bermuda's museums, forts, lighthouses, and architectural treasures, you'll better understand the island's rich cultural tapestry. So, go on a voyage of exploration, exploring these interesting locations and uncovering the tales they contain.

3.6 Adventure Activities: Hiking Trails, Kayaking, Golfing, and More

Bermuda is more than a destination for beachgoers and history aficionados; it's also a playground for adventure seekers! Lace up your hiking boots, grab your paddle, or swing a club, since Bermuda offers a plethora of exciting activities to get your adrenaline racing and fulfil your adventurous side.

Hiking Through Nature's Paradise: Put on your hiking boots and discover Bermuda's vast network of paths. These picturesque routes run through lush woods, dramatic beaches, and secluded coves, providing stunning vistas and opportunities to connect with nature. Here are some popular hikes to consider:

Railway track: This magnificent 1.5-mile track follows the abandoned Bermuda Railway line, providing insight into the island's transportation history and breathtaking ocean views.

South Shore Park walk:
- This gentle 2-mile walk winds across Bermuda's south shore.
- Providing coastal vistas.
- Historical sites.
- Rich flora and wildlife.

Spittal Pond Nature Reserve: Discover Bermuda's distinct environment at the Spittal Pond Nature Reserve. This 32-acre reserve has a network of pathways, a bird sanctuary, and a beautiful saltwater pond.

Image of Spittal Pond Nature Reserve in Bermuda.

Kayaking Adventures: Paddle across Bermuda's turquoise waters to see secret coves, isolated beaches, and amazing marine life from a different angle. Several firms provide kayak rentals and guided trips, catering to people of various skill levels. Imagine kayaking in crystal-clear seas, spotting colourful fish darting under your kayak, and feeling the fresh ocean spray on your face. Pure delight!

Tee Off in Paradise: Golf fans may play on Bermuda's world-class courses. The island is home to numerous championship courses constructed by great golf architects, all providing breathtaking ocean vistas and challenging layouts. Bermuda has golf courses for all ability levels, from the historic Mid-Ocean Club to the picturesque Port Royal Golf Course.

Image of Port Royal Golf Course in Bermuda.

Image of the MidOcean Club, Bermuda.

Beyond the Expected: For those looking for an additional adrenaline thrill, Bermuda has a choice of alternative adventure activities. Coasteering is an exciting experience that involves cliff leaping, swimming, and rock climbing along Bermuda's spectacular coastline. Explore the undersea world with a helmet diving experience, or enjoy a thrilling jet ski excursion around Bermuda's coastline.

An Experience for Every Spirit: Whatever your thrill-seeking level, Bermuda has an experience for you. So, lace up your hiking boots, grab your kayak, or tee off at a championship course. Bermuda provides an extraordinary trip that will leave you excited and eager for more.

3.7 Family Fun: Activities and Attractions for All Ages.

Bermuda is more than simply a romantic vacation or an adventurer's dream; it is also a destination for families looking for spectacular Fun! From gorgeous beaches and historic monuments to interactive museums and exhilarating water sports, Bermuda has something for everyone on the crew.

Beachside Bliss: Bermuda has some of the world's most magnificent beaches, ideal for sandcastles, splashing in the surf, and soaking up the sun. Horseshoe Bay is a family favourite with its distinctive pink sand and tranquil waves. Elbow Beach has a more considerable shoreline length perfect for beach walks and investigating tidal pools. John Smith's Bay offers a relaxing environment with calm seas and services like bathrooms and changing rooms.

John Smith's Bay, Bermuda.

Horseshoe Bay, Bermuda

Elbow Beach, Bermuda.

Underwater Adventures (for Kids): Take your children on a glass-bottom boat excursion to learn about the underwater world. These trips enable you to travel over coral reefs and shipwrecks while seeing colourful fish and other marine life from the comfort of your boat. Many firms provide family-friendly excursions with competent instructors who can answer your children's queries and inspire their interest in the water.

Splashing Fun at the Aquarium, Zoo, and Museum (BAMZ): Families should visit the Bermuda Aquarium, Museum, and Zoo (BAMZ). This interactive facility shows Bermuda's rich marine life, including playful seahorses and magnificent sharks. The zoo includes a variety of terrestrial animals, while the museum displays exhibits about Bermuda's history and culture. Children will like the touch tanks, where they may gently engage with marine animals, and the interactive exhibits depicting Bermuda's natural environment.

Historical Exploration: Take a trip through time by visiting St. George's, Bermuda's UNESCO World Heritage Site. Explore the picturesque alleyways with pastel-coloured houses, visit ancient forts like Fort St. Catherine, and learn about Bermuda's rich history. Many historical sites include interactive exhibitions and events developed expressly to interest young people.

Dockyard Delights: The Royal Naval Dockyard is a thriving activity centre, ideal for a family visit. Explore the ancient Commissioner's House and Clocktower, watch colourful boats arrive and depart from the port, and shop for souvenirs and local crafts. The Dockyard Train, a tiny train that takes visitors on a beautiful complex tour, is a favourite among children.

- **Sailing Adventures:** Set sail on a family-friendly catamaran trip and see Bermuda from a unique viewpoint. These trips include possibilities for swimming, snorkelling, finding secret coves, and eating incredible meals on board. Many cruises cater to families with small children by providing amenities such as life jackets, refreshments, and games to keep them engaged.
- **Beyond the Expected:** Bermuda has several possibilities for families looking for a more adventurous adventure. Take a bike ride along gorgeous trails, bowl at a local alley, or see a movie under the stars at an outdoor theatre. With some forethought, you can construct a Bermuda itinerary that suits everyone's interests and assures a beautiful family trip.

Memories in the Making: Bermuda is the ideal setting for making enduring family memories. So, pack your swimwear and spirit of adventure, and prepare to discover its charm with your loved ones!

Chapter 4: Savoring Bermuda.

4.1 Bermudian Cuisine: Fresh seafood, Indigenous tastes, and worldwide pleasures

"Food is the ingredient that binds us together." — Letty Cottin Pogrebin.

While exploring the gorgeous island of Bermuda, make sure to also go on a food excursion. Bermudian cuisine is a fascinating blend of influences that reflects the island's long history and diversified people. Freshly caught fish, locally produced foods, and foreign tastes offer a distinct and delectable eating experience. Let's tickle your taste buds with these Bermudian must-tries:

A Seafood Symphony: Bermuda, surrounded by blue oceans, has an abundance of fresh seafood. Local delicacies include wahoo, a firm white fish commonly grilled or pan-fried, and mahi-mahi, another tasty fish that may be prepared in various ways. Rockfish, snapper, and tuna are all popular options. Be sure to check out Bermuda's spiny lobster, which is in season from September to March and may be eaten grilled, boiled, or in a luscious lobster bisque.

Fish Chowder - A Bermudian Classic: This rich and savoury stew is Bermuda's national meal. Made with local fish, potatoes, tomatoes, onions, and a dash of Bermudian rum, this chowder is often seasoned with the legendary Outerbridge's Original Sherry Peppers, which provide a smoky spice. Many places offer diverse variants of this traditional dish, so try a couple to pick your favourite.

Traditional Delights: Delights into Bermudian cuisine with classic meals like codfish and potatoes. This meal, commonly served on Sundays, consists of salted codfish cooked with boiled potatoes and eggs and topped with tomato sauce or olive oil. Hoppin' John is another cosy Bermudian classic, made of black-eyed peas and rice with onions and peppers. For a sweet treat, try Bermuda's trademark rum cake, which is thick, savoury and steeped in Bermuda rum.

Ethnic Influences: Reflecting Bermuda's cosmopolitan background, the island offers a diverse range of ethnic cuisines. From Indian curries to Italian pastas to Portuguese favorites and Asian stir-fries, you'll be able to fulfill your multicultural appetites. Many restaurants offer fusion cuisine, which combines Bermudian ingredients with foreign tastes to produce unique and delectable meals.

Farm-Fresh Flavor: Bermuda's devotion to fresh, locally sourced products goes beyond fish. The island has a thriving farm-to-table movement, with many restaurants serving fresh vegetables. Try locally produced lettuces, tomatoes, herbs, and fruits brimming with flavour. Explore Bermuda's farmers' markets for fresh food and locally created jams, jellies, and honey.

A Rum Runner's Paradise: No Bermudian culinary excursion is complete without sampling a delicious rum drink. The black 'n' Stormy, Bermuda's national cocktail, is a simple yet tasty combination of black rum, ginger beer, and lime juice. Another famous Bermudian cocktail is the Rum Swizzle, which combines several rums, fruit juices, and grenadine. With so many rum cocktails, you will indeed discover the ideal island drink.

A gastronomic Adventure Awaits: From fresh seafood delicacies to traditional cuisine and foreign influences, Bermuda's gastronomic culture has something to satisfy every taste. So, go on a delightful adventure, sample the island's delicacies, and create unique dining experiences in Bermuda.

4.2 Dining Out: Restaurants, cafés, bars, and local culinary experiences

Bermuda's thriving food scene is as diversified as its scenery. From exquisite waterfront restaurants to informal cafés and bustling pubs, the island has a great selection of alternatives to satisfy your palate. Let's explore Bermuda's culinary tapestry and find the ideal place to quench your thirst and fulfil your cravings:

Fine Dining with Ocean Views: Bermuda has several fine dining establishments with great food and stunning ocean views for a special occasion or a night of pure indulgence. Treat yourself to a memorable gastronomic experience at

- **Marcus' (Hamilton):** This award-winning restaurant, led by renowned chef Marcus Samuelsson, serves a contemporary twist on Caribbean food with an emphasis on fresh, seasonal ingredients.

- **Coco Reef (Fairmont Southampton):** Enjoy exquisite international cuisine and magnificent South Shore views at Coco Reef. The restaurant's exquisite decor and superb service make it an ideal setting for a romantic evening.

- **L'Auberge (Hamilton):** L'Auberge offers French culinary creativity with spectacular waterfront views. The restaurant's large wine selection and excellent service improve your fine dining experience.

A Taste of Casual Bermuda: For a more relaxed setting, Bermuda has a wealth of casual cafés and restaurants ideal for a leisurely lunch or a laid-back evening. Enjoy fresh seafood dishes, local favourites, and international cuisine at:

- **Wahoo's (Waterfront):** This bustling restaurant on Hamilton's waterfront has a laid-back ambience and serves outstanding Bermudian food. Enjoy fresh seafood, burgers, and a diverse range of local and foreign beers on tap.

- **Bonefish Bar & Grill (Several Locations):** A Bermuda institution, Bonefish provides a casual eating experience emphasizing fresh seafood. Choose from various seafood meals or indulge in their trademark bone-in ribeye.

- **The Pickled Onion (Flatts Village):** Located in Flatts Village, The Pickled Onion has a delightful setting and a delectable menu that combines foreign cuisine with a Bermudian flair.

Bars with Bermudian Charm: Bermuda's evening culture is as lively as its daily activities. After a day of exploring, relax at a local pub or have a refreshing beverage with a view at a waterfront bar.

- **Swizzle Inn (Hamilton):** This famous tavern is a must-see in Bermuda. Try Bermuda's iconic rum drink, the Dark 'n' Stormy, or any of their other rum creations. The Swizzle Inn provides a vibrant environment and the opportunity to meet with locals.

- **Hog Penny Pub (Hamilton):** Another Bermuda institution, Hog Penny Pub provides a traditional atmosphere with a Bermudian twist. Enjoy a variety of beers on tap, pub cuisine, and live music on certain evenings.

- **Huckleberry (Hamilton):** For a more upmarket bar experience, visit Huckleberry. This chic cocktail bar has a unique selection of handmade drinks and a refined atmosphere.

Local Food Experiences: To have a real Bermudian food experience, go outside the restaurants and explore the island's culinary offerings.

- **Friday Night Fish Fry (Hamilton):** Experience Bermuda's rich culture at the Friday Night Fish Fry in Hamilton. This vibrant festival takes place every Friday evening and includes local vendors providing excellent Bermudian dishes such as fish cakes, fried wahoo, and rum cake.
- **Picnic in the Park:** Bring a basket filled with fresh local foods from the Bermuda Farmers' Market and travel to a picturesque park for a delicious picnic. Enjoy the stunning Bermudian countryside while sampling delicious local delicacies.
- **Cooking Class:** Attending a cooking class will teach you the secrets of Bermudian food. Several restaurants and culinary schools provide workshops where you may learn how to make classic foods like fish chowder and rum cake.

Bermuda's food scene caters to all tastes and budgets. So, whether you're looking for a romantic fine-dining experience, a relaxed lunch with a view, or a taste of genuine Bermudian cuisine, you'll discover the ideal place to excite your taste buds and create lasting culinary memories in this magical island paradise.

4.3 Nightlife & Entertainment: Live Music, Pubs, and Island Vibes

"Life begins at night." — *Harvey Firestone.*

Bermuda's dynamic nightlife culture comes to life when the sun sets below the horizon and the sky explodes in colour. The island provides a lovely blend of live music, vibrant bars, and enticing island moods, making it an outstanding experience for night owls and revellers. Let's look at the throbbing centre of Bermuda's after-dark scene.

Live Music Magic: Experience the rhythmic pulse of Bermuda by attending a live music performance. Local and international performers perform in numerous locations over the island, offering a wide selection of musical styles to suit your tastes. Sway to a reggae band's soulful tunes, tap your feet to a dynamic calypso performance, or dance to an exhilarating DJ set. Here are some popular places to hear live music:

- **The Hamilton Princess (Hamilton):** This opulent hotel houses The Crown & Anchor bar, a Bermuda institution noted for its live music scene. You may enjoy a refreshing drink and high-quality entertainment in a typical pub environment.

- **Bonefish Bar & Grill (Several Locations):** While Bonefish is well renowned for its excellent cuisine, it also has live music on some nights. At this casual and energetic establishment, you may have a tasty lunch while listening to toe-tapping music.

- **Berwick Wharf (Dockyard):** Located in the heart of the Royal Naval Dockyard, this waterfront complex hosts live music at different taverns and restaurants weekly. Enjoy live entertainment while taking in the magnificent waterfront views.

Island Pubs & Swizzle Inn Delights: Bermuda has a traditional pub culture, providing a calm setting to unwind with friends and locals after exploring. Sit at the bar of a classic pub and enjoy an excellent beer, a delicious rum drink, and vibrant conversation.

- **Swizzle Inn (Hamilton):** As previously said, this renowned tavern is a must-stop for every tourist to Bermuda. Sample the famous Dark 'n' Stormycocktail, Bermuda's national drink, and enjoy the boisterous environment.

- **Hog Penny Pub (Hamilton)**: Another Bermuda institution, Hog Penny Pub provides a traditional pub experience in a welcoming setting. Enjoy a variety of local and foreign beers on tap, pub food, and the company of other people.

- **The Birdcage (Hamilton):** For a pub experience with a view, visit The Birdcage on the rooftop of the Visitors Center in Hamilton. Sip handmade cocktails and take in the stunning 360-degree views of the city and harbour.

Island Rhythms & Cultural Delights: Learn more about Bermuda's colourful culture by attending one of the island's numerous cultural events. From traditional Gombey parades with colourful costumes and throbbing drumbeats to bustling street festivals and local theatre plays, Bermuda provides a range of opportunities to immerse yourself in the island's rich past. Check local event listings or contact your hotel concierge to find out what's happening during your stay.

Casino Excitement: Test your luck at the Bermuda Casino in the heart of Hamilton. This opulent casino has a variety of tabletop games, slot machines, and opportunities to win large. Whether you're an experienced gambler or simply looking for a fun night out, the Bermuda Casino offers an exciting and elegant ambience.

A Night to Remember: The Bermuda nightlife scene has something for everyone. Soak in the live music, relax at a local bar, learn about the island's unique culture, or try your luck at the casino. Whatever your taste, Bermuda guarantees a fantastic evening of Fun, laughing, and island vibes.

Chapter 5: Beyond The Beaches

5.1 Island Events & Festivals: Cultural Experiences

Bermuda's dynamic spirit is celebrated annually via various events and festivals. Participating in these festivals immerses you in the island's rich culture, throbbing rhythms, and contagious enthusiasm. Let's look at Bermuda's colourful event schedule and see what awaits you:

A Celebration of Heritage: Bermuda Day (May 24th)

Bermuda Day, a national festival commemorating the unofficial start of summer, is regarded as one of Bermuda's largest and most colourful celebrations. The day begins with a vivid procession through Hamilton, with bright floats, vivacious Gombeys dancers in ornate costumes, and marching bands that fill the air with song. Throughout the day, anticipate street festivals, athletic activities like cricket matches, and an overall sense of celebration.

Image of Gombeys Bermuda.

Cup Match Cricket Classic (Thursday and Friday before Bermuda Day):

Cricket fever spreads across Bermuda during the Cup Match Cricket Classic, which takes place two days before Bermuda Day. This traditional rivalry between the island's east and west ends is intense, attracting large audiences and tremendous energy. Join the Fun with locals, eat tasty Bermudian delicacies from food sellers, and soak in the joyful atmosphere.

Harbour Nights (Thursday nights throughout the summer):

Hamilton's Harbour Nights, a weekly summer street celebration, will bring you to life with its vivid energy. The streets become a pedestrian wonderland, filled with local merchants offering crafts, souvenirs, and exquisite Bermudian delights. Live music fills the air, street entertainers demonstrate their skills, and stores remain open late, creating a vibrant and cheerful scene.

Gombey Summer Festival (June-August):

Immerse yourself in Bermuda's rich cultural legacy at the Gombey Summer Festival. This summer event honours the Gombeys, a distinctive Bermudian custom that includes vivid costumes, pulsing drumbeats, and intense dances. Witness lively parades, enthralling performances, and workshops that teach about the history and importance of the Gombeys.

National Heroes Day (June 19th):

Honor Bermuda's national heroes on National Heroes Day, a public holiday observed annually on June 19th. This day honours notable persons who helped build Bermuda's history and culture. Expect church services, special ceremonies, and community celebrations honouring these national heroes.

The Bermuda International Film Festival (Various Dates)

This a must-see for moviegoers. This distinguished festival highlights independent and international films, providing an opportunity to see highly acclaimed projects and interact with creators from all over the globe.

Christmas Cheer in Paradise (November-December):

Celebrate a spectacular Christmas unlike any other in Bermuda. The island becomes a winter paradise, with beautiful lights decorating the streets, carolers filling the air with joyful music, and unique holiday activities held throughout December. Take advantage of the Bermuda National Trust's annual Christmas boat parade, which features a stunning display of lit boats across Hamilton Harbour.

Image of the Bermuda Christmas Boat Parade

A Cultural Journey: Bermuda's events and festivals provide insight into the island's spirit. Participate in these vivid festivals, meet friendly people, and have beautiful experiences that will bring you back for more. So, before your journey, check the event calendar and schedule your

Bermuda excursion to coincide with a festival that catches your attention.

5.2 Travel Etiquette and Customs: Respecting Local Traditions.

As you begin your wonderful trip to Bermuda, here are some vital travel etiquette and traditions to remember for a smooth and polite experience:

Greeting with a Smile: Bermudans are noted for their warm friendliness. A warm grin and a "Good morning" or "Good afternoon" go a long way when dealing with natives.

Respecting Personal Space: Bermudians are amicable but also cherish personal space. Maintain a reasonable distance during talking and refrain from excessive physical greetings.

Bermuda is relaxed and informal, so dress appropriately for any occasion. However, dress more modestly for formal events or trips to sacred locations. When visiting caverns or coves, bring comfortable shoes and a proper swimsuit.

Tipping Etiquette: Tipping is not required in Bermuda, although it is a kind gesture to express gratitude for excellent service. A 10-15% gratuity is usual in restaurants, pubs, and taxis. Hotels often charge a gratuity on top of the bill.

Bargaining: In Bermuda, retail prices are set. Haggling is not expected nor welcomed by retailers.

Photography Etiquette: Getting permission before shooting locals is usually courteous, particularly during cultural events or religious rites. Respect privacy by avoiding taking unwanted photographs.

Respect for the Environment: Bermudans take tremendous pride in their beautiful island. Be a responsible traveller by properly disposing of rubbish, saving water, and protecting animals. Don't touch or disrupt coral reefs or aquatic life.

Relax and Enjoy the Pace: Bermuda prefers a slower pace of life. Be patient when waiting in line or for service. Relax, relax, and enjoy the laid-back island environment.

Learning a Few Bermudian Phrases: While English is the official language, learning a few Bermudian phrases such as "Good morning" ("Good mornin'") or "Thank you" ("Tank you") shows respect for the local culture and will undoubtedly be appreciated by the friendly Bermudians.

Cultural Immersion: Knowing and respecting local traditions and etiquette may improve your Bermudian experience. You'll connect more closely with the welcoming inhabitants, immerse yourself in the island's culture, and make a good impression as a responsible visitor. So pack your bags, enjoy the Bermudian way of life, and prepare to create unforgettable memories on this beautiful island paradise!

Chapter 6: Practical Information.

6.1 Keeping Safe and Healthy: Healthcare, Safety Tips, and Emergency Numbers

Your safety and well-being are critical when on vacation. Here's a simple guide to ensuring a carefree and healthy stay in Bermuda:

Healthcare:

Medical Facilities: Bermuda has outstanding medical facilities and experienced healthcare personnel. The King Edward VII Memorial Hospital is the largest governmental hospital on the island. However, there are also numerous private clinics.

Travel Insurance: Obtain travel insurance before your journey. This policy will cover medical crises, travel cancellations, and other unexpected occurrences.

Prescriptions: If you depend on prescription medications, be sure you have enough supply for your trip. Bring a copy of your doctor's prescription if you need it refilled.

Safety Tips:

Sun Safety: Bermuda's subtropical climate benefits from plenty of sunlight. Wear sunscreen with SPF 30 or higher, sunglasses, and a hat, particularly during peak sun hours (10 a.m. to 4 p.m.).

Ocean Safety:
1. Continuously swim on beaches with lifeguards present.
2. Be wary of rip currents and follow any posted warnings.
3. If you need to become acquainted with the region, avoid swimming alone.

Road Safety: Bermuda follows British road standards, with traffic on the left side of the road. When crossing streets, use care, mainly if the route is small and curving. Renting a scooter is a popular way to explore the island; however, you must always have a valid driver's license and wear a helmet.

Bermuda is usually safe. However, like with any trip location, it is advisable to take common-sense measures. Keep valuables secure, be alert of your surroundings, and avoid going alone in remote regions at night.

Emergency Numbers:

- **Police: Call 911.**
- **Fire/Ambulance: 911.**

- **Bermuda Visitor Services: 1-441-295-5111.**

By following these easy guidelines, you can have a safe and healthy trip to Bermuda. Now that you've equipped yourself with critical knowledge, all that remains is to pack your luggage, book your ticket, and prepare to experience Bermuda's enchantment!

6.2 Communication: Internet access, phone connection, and keeping in contact.

In Bermuda, staying in touch with loved ones back home is easy. Here's an overview of internet access, phone connection, and keeping in contact throughout your island adventure:

Staying online:

- **Widespread Wi-Fi:** Bermuda has a well-developed internet infrastructure. Many hotels, restaurants, cafés, and public locations have free Wi-Fi, enabling you to remain connected and share your Bermudian experiences with the rest of the world.

- **Buying a Local SIM Card:** For more dependable and easily accessible internet connectivity, consider Purchasing a local SIM card from a mobile service provider such as Digicel or CellOne upon arrival. These prepaid SIM cards provide data bundles that meet your needs and budget.

- **Staying Social:** Bermuda's internet connection easily allows you to access social networking platforms, chat applications, and video calling services. Share gorgeous images from your excursions, stay in touch with friends and family back home, and keep them informed on your wonderful Bermudian getaway.

Phone Connectivity:

- **International Roaming:** Before you go, check with your cell service provider regarding international roaming rates. Roaming costs vary according to your provider and plan. Some carriers provide Wi-Fi calling options, which might be more cost-effective for making calls.

- **Local SIM Card for Calls:** The local SIM card you buy for internet access may often be used to make phone calls. This might be a cost-effective way to remain in contact with loved ones who aren't available via online messaging.

Staying In Touch:

- **Several free Wi-Fi** calling applications, such as WhatsApp or Viber, enable you to make voice and video conversations over a Wi-Fi connection.

This is an excellent method to keep in touch with friends and family without paying roaming costs.

- **Calling Cards:** While calling cards are no longer as prevalent as they used to be, they may still be used to make calls, particularly if you anticipate having a restricted internet connection. These may be obtained at convenience shops or online before your travel.

Keeping Connected with Ease: Bermuda offers broad Wi-Fi access and a variety of mobile communication choices, making keeping in contact with loved ones back home simple. So document your Bermudian vacation, share your stories, and let everyone know you're having a great time on this beautiful island paradise!

6.3 Sustainable Travel: Eco-Friendly Practices for Exploring Bermuda

Bermuda greets you with open arms, gorgeous beaches, and abundant natural beauty. As a responsible tourist, you must tread softly and adopt sustainable behaviours to guarantee that the island's charm lasts for future generations. Here's how you can help make Bermuda greener:

Reduce, Reuse, and Recycle: This ageless adage also applies to your Bermudian experience. To prevent single-use plastics, pack reusable water bottles. Use hotel commodities like towels and linens wisely, and try to reuse them wherever feasible. Many Bermuda hotels have implemented environmental measures, such as providing recycling bins for visitors. Do your part and dispose of rubbish properly.

Embrace Public Transportation: Bermuda has a well-developed public transportation system that includes buses, ferries, and moped rentals. Choosing these choices decreases your carbon impact compared to hiring a private automobile during your trip. Consider getting a multi-day transit ticket for economical and environmentally beneficial exploring.

Explore by Bike or Scooter: For a more adventurous and environmentally responsible way to see the island, hire a bicycle or an electric scooter. These choices enable you to enjoy Bermuda's gorgeous surroundings at your leisure while reducing your environmental impact. Remember to wear a helmet and obey traffic laws for a safe and fun ride.

Respect the Delicate Ecosystem: Bermuda's coral reefs and marine life are critical to the island's ecology. When snorkelling or diving, be aware of your surroundings. Avoid touching or standing on coral reefs, and properly dispose of garbage. Encourage local eco-tours that highlight ethical tourist activities.

Embrace Local and Seasonal Produce: Enjoy Bermuda's exquisite tastes using fresh, local foods. Farmers' markets are excellent places to purchase seasonal fruits, vegetables, and locally produced seafood.

Buying local produce minimizes food transportation's carbon impact while supporting Bermuda's agricultural sector.

Minimize Water Consumption: Although Bermuda's water is safe, water conservation is critical. Take shorter showers, reuse towels wherever feasible, and avoid running the faucet excessively. Remember that Bermuda is a semiarid island; therefore, every drop matters!

Support Sustainable Firms: Many Bermudian firms are devoted to environmentally responsible operations. Look for hotels and restaurants that promote sustainability activities such as renewable energy use, trash reduction, and local conservation efforts. By selecting these establishments, you convey a good message and promote ethical tourist practices.

Leave No Trace:
1. When visiting Bermuda's gorgeous beaches, parks, and natural treasures, obey the "Leave No Trace" guidelines.
2. Pack out all rubbish, be respectful to animals, and minimize your environmental effects.
3. Leave the island as pristine as you found it so future generations might enjoy its beauty.

By implementing these sustainable practices into your Bermudian journey, you positively impact the island's ecosystem and safeguard its long-term beauty. Remember that even little adjustments may have a significant effect. So, embrace responsible tourism,

explore mindfully, and leave a lasting good impression on this enchanting island paradise.

Chapter 7: Appendix
A1. Maps of Bermuda.

A2. Bermudian Phrases

Greetings:

- Wopnin' (Whuppin') is a shorter form of "What's happening?" and is a typical greeting in Bermuda.
- Good Morning (maanin').
- Good evening (eevin). - Good evening.
- How're you doing? - How are you?

Responses:

- A'right (Iright) - I am OK.
- I am doing well, so I cannot complain.
- Excellent (top notch).
- Expressing gratitude:
- Thank you (yuh) means thank you.
- No issue (no problem). You are welcome.
- You're welcome.

Other useful phrases:
- Excuse me (excuse me).
- Would you please...? (Could you please...?) Could you please...?
- Sorry (sorry).
- That's nice. - That is nice.
- Lovely (luvly). - Lovely.
- Beautiful (incredible) - Beautiful.
- Chingas! - Wow! (An exclamation of surprise or happiness).

- Ace boy/girl - A close buddy (may be used thoughtfully and humorously).
- Greeze - A big lunch.

Please keep in mind that the Bermudian accent has distinct pronunciation and cadence. These words will give you basic comprehension and allow you to feel the local character. Don't be scared to try them out, and have Fun learning the language!

Made in the USA
Columbia, SC
28 October 2024

45179317R00054